T. S. ELIOT
Old Possum's Book of Practical Cats

with decorations by
NICOLAS BENTLEY

ff

faber and faber

First published in 1939
by Faber and Faber Limited
3 Queen Square London WC1N 3AU

This paperback edition first published in 2006

Photoset by Wilmaset Ltd. Wirral
Printed in England by Mackays of Chatham PLC
All rights reserved

A CIP record for this book is
available from the British Library

ISBN 978-0-571-23520-9
ISBN 0-571-23520-4

2 4 6 8 10 9 7 5 3 1

This book is respectfully dedicated to those friends who have assisted its composition by their encouragement, criticism and suggestions: and in particular to Mr T. E. Faber, Miss Alison Tandy, Miss Susan Wolcott, Miss Susanna Morley, and the Man in White Spats.

O.P.

Contents

The Naming of Cats 1
The Old Gumbie Cat 5
Growltiger's Last Stand 7
The Rum Tum Tugger 11
The Song of the Jellicles 15
Mungojerrie and Rumpelteazer 17
Old Deuteronomy 21
The Pekes and the Pollicles 23
Mr Mistoffelees 27
Macavity: The Mystery Cat 31
Gus: The Theatre Cat 35
Bustopher Jones: The Cat about Town 39
Skimbleshanks: The Railway Cat 41
The Ad-dressing of Cats 45
Cat Morgan Introduces Himself 49

The Naming of Cats

The Naming of Cats is a difficult matter,
　　It isn't just one of your holiday games;
You may think at first I'm as mad as a hatter
When I tell you, a cat must have THREE DIFFERENT
　　NAMES.
First of all, there's the name that the family use daily,
　　Such as Peter, Augustus, Alonzo or James,
Such as Victor or Jonathan, George or Bill Bailey —
　　All of them sensible everyday names.
There are fancier names if you think they sound sweeter,
　　Some for the gentlemen, some for the dames:
Such as Plato, Admetus, Electra, Demeter —
　　But all of them sensible everyday names.
But I tell you, a cat needs a name that's particular,
　　A name that's peculiar, and more dignified,
Else how can he keep up his tail perpendicular,
　　Or spread out his whiskers, or cherish his pride?
Of names of this kind, I can give you a quorum,
　　Such as Munkustrap, Quaxo, or Coricopat,
Such as Bombalurina, or else Jellylorum —
　　Names that never belong to more than one cat.
But above and beyond there's still one name left over,
　　And that is the name that you never will guess;
The name that no human research can discover —
　　But THE CAT HIMSELF KNOWS, and will never confess.
When you notice a cat in profound meditation,
　　The reason, I tell you, is always the same:

His mind is engaged in a rapt contemplation
  Of the thought, of the thought, of the thought of his
      name:
    His ineffable effable
    Effanineffable
Deep and inscrutable singular Name.

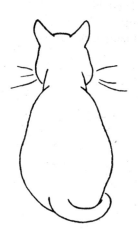

The Old Gumbie Cat

I have a Gumbie Cat in mind, her name is Jennyanydots;
Her coat is of the tabby kind, with tiger stripes and
    leopard spots.
All day she sits upon the stair or on the steps or on the
    mat:
She sits and sits and sits and sits — and that's what makes
    a Gumbie Cat!

    But when the day's hustle and bustle is done,
    Then the Gumbie Cat's work is but hardly begun.
    And when all the family's in bed and asleep,
    She slips down the stairs to the basement to creep.
    She is deeply concerned with the ways of the mice —
    Their behaviour's not good and their manners not nice;
    So when she has got them lined up on the matting,
    She teaches them music, crocheting and tatting.

I have a Gumbie Cat in mind, her name is Jennyanydots;
Her equal would be hard to find, she likes the warm and
    sunny spots.
All day she sits beside the hearth or in the sun or on my
    hat:
She sits and sits and sits and sits — and that's what makes
    a Gumbie Cat!

    But when the day's hustle and bustle is done,
    Then the Gumbie Cat's work is but hardly begun.
    As she finds that the mice will not ever keep quiet,
    She is sure it is due to irregular diet
    And believing that nothing is done without trying,
    She sets straight to work with her baking and frying.

She makes them a mouse-cake of bread and dried peas,
And a *beautiful* fry of lean bacon and cheese.

I have a Gumbie Cat in mind, her name is Jennyanydots;
The curtain-cord she likes to wind, and tie it into sailor-
    knots.
She sits upon the window-sill, or anything that's smooth
    and flat:
She sits and sits and sits and sits — and that's what makes
    a Gumbie Cat!

But when the day's hustle and bustle is done,
Then the Gumbie Cat's work is but hardly begun.
She thinks that the cockroaches just need employment
To prevent them from idle and wanton destroyment.
So she's formed, from that lot of disorderly louts,
A troop of well-disciplined helpful boy-scouts,
With a purpose in life and a good deed to do —
And she's even created a Beetles' Tattoo.

So for Old Gumbie Cats let us now give three cheers —
On whom well-ordered households depend, it appears.

Growltiger's Last Stand

Growltiger was a Bravo Cat, who travelled on a barge:
In fact he was the roughest cat that ever roamed at large.
From Gravesend up to Oxford he pursued his evil aims,
Rejoicing in his title of 'The Terror of the Thames'.

His manners and appearance did not calculate to please;
His coat was torn and seedy, he was baggy at the knees;
One ear was somewhat missing, no need to tell you why,
And he scowled upon a hostile world from one
    forbidding eye.

The cottagers of Rotherhithe knew something of his fame;
At Hammersmith and Putney people shuddered at his
    name.
They would fortify the hen-house, lock up the silly goose,
When the rumour ran along the shore: GROWLTIGER'S
ON THE LOOSE!

Woe to the weak canary, that fluttered from its cage;
Woe to the pampered Pekinese, that faced Growltiger's
    rage;
Woe to the bristly Bandicoot, that lurks on foreign ships,
And woe to any Cat with whom Growltiger came to
    grips!

But most to Cats of foreign race his hatred had been
    vowed;
To Cats of foreign name and race no quarter was allowed.
The Persian and the Siamese regarded him with fear —
Because it was a Siamese had mauled his missing ear.

Now on a peaceful summer night, all nature seemed at
    play,
The tender moon was shining bright, the barge at
    Molesey lay.
All in the balmy moonlight it lay rocking on the tide —
And Growltiger was disposed to show his sentimental
    side.

His bucko mate, GRUMBUSKIN, long since had
    disappeared,
For to the Bell at Hampton he had gone to wet his beard;
And his bosun, TUMBLEBRUTUS, he too had stol'n
    away —
In the yard behind the Lion he was prowling for his prey.

In the forepeak of the vessel Growltiger sate alone,
Concentrating his attention on the Lady GRIDDLEBONE.
And his raffish crew were sleeping in their barrels and
    their bunks —
As the Siamese came creeping in their sampans and their
    junks.

Growltiger had no eye or ear for aught but Griddlebone,
And the Lady seemed enraptured by his manly baritone,
Disposed to relaxation, and awaiting no surprise —
But the moonlight shone reflected from a hundred bright
    blue eyes.

And closer still and closer the sampans circled round,
And yet from all the enemy there was not heard a sound.
The lovers sang their last duet, in danger of their lives —
For the foe was armed with toasting forks and cruel
    carving knives.

Then GILBERT gave the signal to his fierce Mongolian
horde;
With a frightful burst of fireworks the Chinks they
swarmed aboard.
Abandoning their sampans, and their pullaways and
junks,
They battened down the hatches on the crew within their
bunks.

Then Griddlebone she gave a screech, for she was badly
skeered;
I am sorry to admit it, but she quickly disappeared.
She probably escaped with ease, I'm sure she was not
drowned —
But a serried ring of flashing steel Growltiger did
surround.

The ruthless foe pressed forward, in stubborn rank on
rank;
Growltiger to his vast surprise was forced to walk the
plank.
He who a hundred victims had driven to that drop,
At the end of all his crimes was forced to go ker-flip,
ker-flop.

Oh there was joy in Wapping when the news flew
through the land;
At Maidenhead and Henley there was dancing on the
strand.
Rats were roasted whole at Brentford, and at Victoria
Dock,
And a day of celebration was commanded in Bangkok.

The Rum Tum Tugger

The Rum Tum Tugger is a Curious Cat:
If you offer him pheasant he would rather have grouse.
If you put him in a house he would much prefer a flat,
If you put him in a flat then he'd rather have a house.
If you set him on a mouse then he only wants a rat,
If you set him on a rat then he'd rather chase a mouse.
Yes the Rum Tum Tugger is a Curious Cat —
  And there isn't any call for me to shout it:
    For he will do
    As he do do
      And there's no doing anything about it!

The Rum Tum Tugger is a terrible bore:
When you let him in, then he wants to be out;
He's always on the wrong side of every door,
And as soon as he's at home, then he'd like to get about.
He likes to lie in the bureau drawer,
But he makes such a fuss if he can't get out.
Yes the Rum Tum Tugger is a Curious Cat —
  And it isn't any use for you to doubt it:
    For he will do
    As he do do
      And there's no doing anything about it!

The Rum Tum Tugger is a curious beast:
His disobliging ways are a matter of habit.
If you offer him fish then he always wants a feast;
When there isn't any fish then he won't eat rabbit.
If you offer him cream then he sniffs and sneers,
For he only likes what he finds for himself;
So you'll catch him in it right up to the ears,

If you put it away on the larder shelf.
The Rum Tum Tugger is artful and knowing,
The Rum Tum Tugger doesn't care for a cuddle;
But he'll leap on your lap in the middle of your sewing,
For there's nothing he enjoys like a horrible muddle.
Yes the Rum Tum Tugger is a Curious Cat —
  And there isn't any need for me to spout it:
    For he will do
    As he do do
      And there's no doing anything about it!

The Song of the Jellicles

Jellicle Cats come out to-night
Jellicle Cats come one come all:
The Jellicle Moon is shining bright —
Jellicles come to the Jellicle Ball.

Jellicle Cats are black and white,
Jellicle Cats are rather small;
Jellicle Cats are merry and bright,
And pleasant to hear when they caterwaul.
Jellicle Cats have cheerful faces,
Jellicle Cats have bright black eyes;
They like to practise their airs and graces
And wait for the Jellicle Moon to rise.

Jellicle Cats develop slowly,
Jellicle Cats are not too big;
Jellicle Cats are roly-poly,
They know how to dance a gavotte and a jig.
Until the Jellicle Moon appears
They make their toilette and take their repose:
Jellicles wash behind their ears,
Jellicles dry between their toes.

Jellicle Cats are white and black,
Jellicle Cats are of moderate size;
Jellicles jump like a jumping-jack,
Jellicle Cats have moonlit eyes.
They're quiet enough in the morning hours,
They're quiet enough in the afternoon,
Reserving their terpsichorean powers
To dance by the light of the Jellicle Moon.

Jellicle Cats are black and white,
Jellicle Cats (as I said) are small;
If it happens to be a stormy night
They will practise a caper or two in the hall.
If it happens the sun is shining bright
You would say they had nothing to do at all:
They are resting and saving themselves to be right
For the Jellicle Moon and the Jellicle Ball.

Mungojerrie and Rumpelteazer

Mungojerrie and Rumpelteazer were a very notorious
  couple of cats.
As knockabout clowns, quick-change comedians,
  tight-rope walkers and acrobats
They had an extensive reputation. They made their home
  in Victoria Grove —
That was merely their centre of operation, for they were
  incurably given to rove.
They were very well known in Cornwall Gardens, in
  Launceston Place and in Kensington Square —
They had really a little more reputation than a couple of
  cats can very well bear.

  If the area window was found ajar
  And the basement looked like a field of war,
  If a tile or two came loose on the roof,
  Which presently ceased to be waterproof,
  If the drawers were pulled out from the bedroom
    chests,
  And you couldn't find one of your winter vests,
  Or after supper one of the girls
  Suddenly missed her Woolworth pearls:
Then the family would say: 'It's that horrible cat!
It was Mungojerrie — or Rumpelteazer!' — And most of
  the time they left it at that.

Mungojerrie and Rumpelteazer had a very unusual gift of
   the gab.
They were highly efficient cat-burglars as well, and
   remarkably smart at a smash-and-grab.
They made their home in Victoria Grove. They had no
   regular occupation.
They were plausible fellows, and liked to engage a
   friendly policeman in conversation.

   When the family assembled for Sunday dinner,
   With their minds made up that they wouldn't get
      thinner
   On Argentine joint, potatoes and greens,
   And the cook would appear from behind the scenes
   And say in a voice that was broken with sorrow:
   'I'm afraid you must wait and have dinner *tomorrow*!
   For the joint has gone from the oven — like that!'
Then the family would say: 'It's that horrible cat!
It was Mungojerrie — or Rumpelteazer!' — And most of
   the time they left it at that.

Mungojerrie and Rumpelteazer had a wonderful way of
   working together.
And some of the time you would say it was luck, and
   some of the time you would say it was weather.
They would go through the house like a hurricane, and
   no sober person could take his oath
Was it Mungojerrie — or Rumpelteazer? or could you
   have sworn that it mightn't be both?

   And when you heard a dining-room smash
   Or up from the pantry there came a loud crash
   Or down from the library came a loud *ping*
   From a vase which was commonly said to be Ming —

Then the family would say: 'Now which was which cat?
It was Mungojerrie! AND Rumpelteazer!' — And there's
  nothing at all to be done about that!

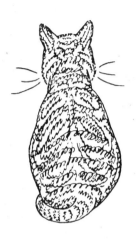

Old Deuteronomy

Old Deuteronomy's lived a long time;
 He's a Cat who has lived many lives in succession.
He was famous in proverb and famous in rhyme
 A long while before Queen Victoria's accession.
Old Deuteronomy's buried nine wives
 And more — I am tempted to say, ninety-nine;
And his numerous progeny prospers and thrives
 And the village is proud of him in his decline.
At the sight of that placid and bland physiognomy,
 When he sits in the sun on the vicarage wall,
The Oldest Inhabitant croaks: 'Well, of all . . .
 Things . . . Can it be . . . really! . . . No! . . . Yes! . . .
 Ho! hi!
 Oh, my eye!
My sight may be failing, but yet I confess
I *believe* it is Old Deuteronomy!'

Old Deuteronomy sits in the street,
 He sits in the High Street on market day;
The bullocks may bellow, the sheep they may bleat,
 But the dogs and the herdsmen will turn them away.
The cars and the lorries run over the kerb,
 And the villagers put up a notice: ROAD CLOSED —
So that nothing untoward may chance to disturb
 Deuteronomy's rest when he feels so disposed
Or when he's engaged in domestic economy:

And the Oldest Inhabitant croaks: 'Well, of all . . .
Things . . . Can it be . . . really! . . . No! . . . Yes! . . .
 Ho! hi!
 Oh, my eye!
I'm deaf of an ear now, but yet I can guess
That the cause of the trouble is Old Deuteronomy!'

Old Deuteronomy lies on the floor
 Of the Fox and French Horn for his afternoon sleep;
And when the men say: 'There's just time for one more,'
 Then the landlady from her back parlour will peep
And say: 'Now then, out you go, by the back door,
 For Old Deuteronomy mustn't be woken —
I'll have the police if there's any uproar' —
 And out they all shuffle, without a word spoken.
The digestive repose of that feline's gastronomy
 Must never be broken, whatever befall:
And the Oldest Inhabitant croaks: 'Well, of all . . .
 Things . . . Can it be . . . really! . . . Yes! . . . No! . . .
 Ho! hi!
 Oh, my eye!
My legs may be tottery, I must go slow
And be careful of Old Deuteronomy!'

Of the Awefull Battle
of the Pekes and the Pollicles

TOGETHER WITH SOME ACCOUNT
OF THE PARTICIPATION
OF THE PUGS AND THE POMS, AND THE
INTERVENTION OF THE GREAT RUMPUSCAT

The Pekes and the Pollicles, everyone knows,
Are proud and implacable passionate foes;
It is always the same, wherever one goes.
And the Pugs and the Poms, although most people say
That they do not like fighting, will often display
Every symptom of wanting to join in the fray.
And they
              Bark bark bark bark
              Bark bark BARK BARK
      Until you can hear them all over the Park.

Now on the occasion of which I shall speak
Almost nothing had happened for nearly a week
(And that's a long time for a Pol or a Peke).
The big Police Dog was away from his beat —
I don't know the reason, but most people think
He'd slipped into the Bricklayer's Arms for a drink —
And no one at all was about on the street
When a Peke and a Pollicle happened to meet.
They did not advance, or exactly retreat,
But they glared at each other, and scraped their hind feet,
And started to
              Bark bark bark bark
              Bark bark BARK BARK
      Until you can hear them all over the Park.

Now the Peke, although people may say what they
    please,
Is no British Dog, but a Heathen Chinese.
And so all the Pekes, when they heard the uproar,
Some came to the window, some came to the door;
There were surely a dozen, more likely a score.
And together they started to grumble and wheeze
In their huffery-snuffery Heathen Chinese.
But a terrible din is what Pollicles like,
For your Pollicle Dog is a dour Yorkshire tyke,
And his braw Scottish cousins are snappers and biters,
And every dog-jack of them notable fighters;
And so they stepped out, with their pipers in order,
Playing *When the Blue Bonnets Came Over the Border*.
Then the Pugs and the Poms held no longer aloof,
But some from the balcony, some from the roof,
Joined in
To the din
With a

> Bark bark bark bark
> Bark bark BARK BARK
Until you can hear them all over the Park.

Now when these bold heroes together assembled,
The traffic all stopped, and the Underground trembled,
And some of the neighbours were so much afraid
That they started to ring up the Fire Brigade.
When suddenly, up from a small basement flat,
Why who should stalk out but the GREAT RUMPUSCAT.
His eyes were like fireballs fearfully blazing,
He gave a great yawn, and his jaws were amazing;
And when he looked out through the bars of the area,
You never saw anything fiercer or hairier.

And what with the glare of his eyes and his yawning,
The Pekes and the Pollicles quickly took warning.
He looked at the sky and he gave a great leap —
And they every last one of them scattered like sheep.

And when the Police Dog returned to his beat,
There wasn't a single one left in the street.

Mr Mistoffelees

You ought to know Mr Mistoffelees!
The Original Conjuring Cat —
(There can be no doubt about that).
Please listen to me and don't scoff. All his
Inventions are off his own bat.
There's no such Cat in the metropolis;
He holds all the patent monopolies
For performing surprising illusions
And creating eccentric confusions.
    At prestidigitation
        And at legerdemain
    He'll defy examination
        And deceive you again.
The greatest magicians have something to learn
From Mr Mistoffelees' Conjuring Turn.
Presto!
    Away we go!
        And we all say: OH!
            Well I never!
            Was there ever
            A Cat so clever
                As Magical Mr Mistoffelees!

He is quiet and small, he is black
From his ears to the tip of his tail;
He can creep through the tiniest crack
He can walk on the narrowest rail.
He can pick any card from a pack,
He is equally cunning with dice;
He is always deceiving you into believing

That he's only hunting for mice.
　　He can play any trick with a cork
　　　Or a spoon and a bit of fish-paste;
　　If you look for a knife or a fork
　　　And you think it is merely misplaced —
You have seen it one moment, and then it is *gawn*!
But you'll find it next week lying out on the lawn.
　　And we all say: OH!
　　　Well I never!
　　　Was there ever
　　　A Cat so clever
　　　　As Magical Mr Mistoffelees!

His manner is vague and aloof,
You would think there was nobody shyer —
But his voice has been heard on the roof
When he was curled up by the fire.
And he's sometimes been heard by the fire
When he was about on the roof —
(At least we all *heard* somebody who purred)
Which is incontestable proof
　　Of his singular magical powers:
　　　And I have known the family to call
　　Him in from the garden for hours,
　　　While he was asleep in the hall.
And not long ago this phenomenal Cat
Produced *seven kittens* right out of a hat!
　　And we all said: OH!
　　　Well I never!
　　　Did you ever
　　　Know a Cat so clever
　　　　As Magical Mr Mistoffelees!

Macavity: The Mystery Cat

Macavity's a Mystery Cat: he's called the Hidden Paw —
For he's the master criminal who can defy the Law.
He's the bafflement of Scotland Yard, the Flying Squad's
 despair:
For when they reach the scene of crime — *Macavity's not
 there*!

Macavity, Macavity, there's no one like Macavity,
He's broken every human law, he breaks the law of
 gravity.
His powers of levitation would make a fakir stare,
And when you reach the scene of crime — *Macavity's not
 there*!
You may seek him in the basement, you may look up in
 the air —
But I tell you once and once again, *Macavity's not there*!

Macavity's a ginger cat, he's very tall and thin;
You would know him if you saw him, for his eyes are
 sunken in.
His brow is deeply lined with thought, his head is highly
 domed;
His coat is dusty from neglect, his whiskers are
 uncombed.
He sways his head from side to side, with movements like
 a snake;
And when you think he's half asleep, he's always wide
 awake.

Macavity, Macavity, there's no one like Macavity,
For he's a fiend in feline shape, a monster of depravity.
You may meet him in a by-street, you may see him in the
    square —
But when a crime's discovered, then *Macavity's not there*!

He's outwardly respectable. (They say he cheats at cards.)
And his footprints are not found in any file of Scotland
    Yard's.
And when the larder's looted, or the jewel-case is rifled,
Or when the milk is missing, or another Peke's been
    stifled,
Or the greenhouse glass is broken, and the trellis past
    repair —
Ay, there's the wonder of the thing! *Macavity's not there*!

And when the Foreign Office find a Treaty's gone astray,
Or the Admiralty lose some plans and drawings by the
    way,
There may be a scrap of paper in the hall or on the stair —
But it's useless to investigate — *Macavity's not there*!
And when the loss has been disclosed, the Secret Service
    say:
'It *must* have been Macavity!' — but he's a mile away.
You'll be sure to find him resting, or a-licking of his
    thumbs,
Or engaged in doing complicated long division sums.

Macavity, Macavity, there's no one like Macavity,
There never was a Cat of such deceitfulness and suavity.
He always has an alibi, and one or two to spare:
At whatever time the deed took place — MACAVITY
    WASN'T THERE!

And they say that all the Cats whose wicked deeds are
   widely known
(I might mention Mungojerrie, I might mention
   Griddlebone)
Are nothing more than agents for the Cat who all the time
Just controls their operations: the Napoleon of Crime!

Gus: The Theatre Cat

Gus is the Cat at the Theatre Door.
His name, as I ought to have told you before,
Is really Asparagus. That's such a fuss
To pronounce, that we usually call him just Gus.
His coat's very shabby, he's thin as a rake,
And he suffers from palsy that makes his paw shake.
Yet he was, in his youth, quite the smartest of Cats —
But no longer a terror to mice and to rats.
For he isn't the Cat that he was in his prime;
Though his name was quite famous, he says, in its time.
And whenever he joins his friends at their club
(Which takes place at the back of the neighbouring pub)
He loves to regale them, if someone else pays,
With anecdotes drawn from his palmiest days.
For he once was a Star of the highest degree —
He has acted with Irving, he's acted with Tree.
And he likes to relate his success on the Halls,
Where the Gallery once gave him seven cat-calls.
But his grandest creation, as he loves to tell,
Was Firefrorefiddle, the Fiend of the Fell.

'I have played', so he says, 'every possible part,
And I use to know seventy speeches by heart.
I'd extemporize back-chat, I knew how to gag,
And I knew how to let the cat out of the bag.
I knew how to act with my back and my tail;
With an hour of rehearsal, I never could fail.
I'd a voice that would soften the hardest of hearts,
Whether I took the lead, or in character parts.
I have sat by the bedside of poor Little Nell;

When the Curfew was rung, then I swung on the bell.
In the Pantomime season I never fell flat
And I once understudied Dick Whittington's Cat.
But my grandest creation, as history will tell,
Was Firefrorefiddle, the Fiend of the Fell.'

Then, if someone will give him a toothful of gin,
He will tell how he once played a part in *East Lynne*.
At a Shakespeare performance he once walked on pat,
When some actor suggested the need for a cat.
He once played a Tiger — could do it again —
Which an Indian Colonel pursued down a drain.
And he thinks that he still can, much better than most,
Produce blood-curdling noises to bring on the Ghost.
And he once crossed the stage on a telegraph wire,
To rescue a child when a house was on fire.
And he says: 'Now, these kittens, they do not get trained
As we did in the days when Victoria reigned.
They never get drilled in a regular troupe,
And they think they are smart, just to jump through a
    hoop.'
And he'll say, as he scratches himself with his claws,
'Well, the Theatre's certainly not what it was.
These modern productions are all very well,
But there's nothing to equal, from what I hear tell,
    That moment of mystery
    When I made history
As Firefrorefiddle, the Fiend of the Fell.'

Bustopher Jones: The Cat about Town

Bustopher Jones is *not* skin and bones —
In fact, he's remarkably fat.
He doesn't haunt pubs — he has eight or nine clubs,
For he's the St James's Street Cat!
He's the Cat we all greet as he walks down the street
In his coat of fastidious black:
No commonplace mousers have such well-cut trousers
Or such an impeccable back.
In the whole of St James's the smartest of names is
The name of this Brummell of Cats;
And we're all of us proud to be nodded or bowed to
By Bustopher Jones in white spats!

His visits are occasional to the *Senior Educational*
And it is against the rules
For any one Cat to belong both to that
And the *Joint Superior Schools.*
For a similar reason, when game is in season
He is found, not at *Fox's*, but *Blimp's*;
But he's frequently seen at the gay *Stage and Screen*
Which is famous for winkles and shrimps.
In the season of venison he gives his ben'son
To the *Pothunter's* succulent bones;
And just before noon's not a moment too soon
To drop in for a drink at the *Drones.*
When he's seen in a hurry there's probably curry
At the *Siamese* — or at the *Glutton*;
If he looks full of gloom then he's lunched at the *Tomb*
On cabbage, rice pudding and mutton.

So, much in this way, passes Bustopher's day —
At one club or another he's found.
It can cause no surprise that under our eyes
He has grown unmistakably round.
He's a twenty-five pounder, or I am a bounder,
And he's putting on weight every day:
But he's so well preserved because he's observed
All his life a routine, so he'll say.
And (to put it in rhyme) 'I shall last out my time'
Is the word of this stoutest of Cats.
It must and it shall be Spring in Pall Mall
While Bustopher Jones wears white spats!

Skimbleshanks: The Railway Cat

There's a whisper down the line at 11.39
When the Night Mail's ready to depart,
Saying 'Skimble where is Skimble has he gone to hunt the
    thimble?
We must find him or the train can't start.'
All the guards and all the porters and the stationmaster's
    daughters
They are searching high and low,
Saying 'Skimble where is Skimble for unless he's very
    nimble
Then the Night Mail just can't go.'
At 11.42 then the signal's nearly due
And the passengers are frantic to a man —
Then Skimble will appear and he'll saunter to the rear:
He's been busy in the luggage van!
    He gives one flash of his glass-green eyes
        And the signal goes 'All Clear!'
    And we're off at last for the northern part
        Of the Northern Hemisphere!

You may say that by and large it is Skimble who's in
    charge
Of the Sleeping Car Express.
From the driver and the guards to the bagmen playing
    cards
He will supervise them all, more or less.
Down the corridor he paces and examines all the faces
Of the travellers in the First and in the Third;
He establishes control by a regular patrol
And he'd know at once if anything occurred.

He will watch you without winking and he sees what you
    are thinking
And it's certain that he doesn't approve
Of hilarity and riot, so the folk are very quiet
When Skimble is about and on the move.
    You can play no pranks with Skimbleshanks!
        He's a Cat that cannot be ignored;
    So nothing goes wrong on the Northern Mail
        When Skimbleshanks is aboard.

Oh it's very pleasant when you have found your little den
With your name written up on the door.
And the berth is very neat with a newly folded sheet
And there's not a speck of dust on the floor.
There is every sort of light — you can make it dark or
    bright;
There's a button that you turn to make a breeze.
There's a funny little basin you're supposed to wash your
    face in
And a crank to shut the window if you sneeze.
Then the guard looks in politely and will ask you very
    brightly
'Do you like your morning tea weak or strong?'
But Skimble's just behind him and was ready to remind
    him,
For Skimble won't let anything go wrong.
    And when you creep into your cosy berth
        And pull up the counterpane,
You are bound to admit that it's very nice
To know that you won't be bothered by mice —
You can leave all that to the Railway Cat,
    The Cat of the Railway Train!

In the middle of the night he is always fresh and bright;
Every now and then he has a cup of tea
With perhaps a drop of Scotch while he's keeping on the
   watch,
Only stopping here and there to catch a flea.
You were fast asleep at Crewe and so you never knew
That he was walking up and down the station;
You were sleeping all the while he was busy at Carlisle,
Where he greets the stationmaster with elation.
But you saw him at Dumfries, where he summons the
   police
If there's anything they ought to know about:
When you get to Gallowgate there you do not have to
   wait —
For Skimbleshanks will help you to get out!
   He gives you a wave of his long brown tail
      Which says: 'I'll see you again!
   You'll meet without fail on the Midnight Mail
      The Cat of the Railway Train.'

The Ad-dressing of Cats

You've read of several kinds of Cat,
And my opinion now is that
You should need no interpreter
To understand their character.
You now have learned enough to see
That Cats are much like you and me
And other people whom we find
Possessed of various types of mind.
For some are sane and some are mad
And some are good and some are bad
And some are better, some are worse —
But all may be described in verse.
You've seen them both at work and games,
And learnt about their proper names,
Their habits and their habitat:
But
    How would you ad-dress a Cat?

So first, your memory I'll jog,
And say: A CAT IS NOT A DOG.

Now Dogs pretend they like to fight;
They often bark, more seldom bite;
But yet a Dog is, on the whole,
What you would call a simple soul.
Of course I'm not including Pekes,
And such fantastic canine freaks.
The usual Dog about the Town
Is much inclined to play the clown,
And far from showing too much pride
Is frequently undignified.

He's very easily taken in —
Just chuck him underneath the chin
Or slap his back or shake his paw,
And he will gambol and guffaw.
He's such an easy-going lout,
He'll answer any hail or shout.

Again I must remind you that
A Dog's a Dog — A CAT'S A CAT.

With Cats, some say, one rule is true:
Don't speak till you are spoken to.
Myself, I do not hold with that —
I say, you should ad-dress a Cat.
But always keep in mind that he
Resents familiarity.
I bow, and taking off my hat,
Ad-dress him in this form: O CAT!
But if he is the Cat next door,
Whom I have often met before
(He comes to see me in my flat)
I greet him with an OOPSA CAT!
I've heard them call him James Buz-James —
But we've not got so far as names.
Before a Cat will condescend
To treat you as a trusted friend,
Some little token of esteem
Is needed, like a dish of cream;
And you might now and then supply
Some caviare, or Strassburg Pie,
Some potted grouse, or salmon paste —
He's sure to have his personal taste.
(I know a Cat, who makes a habit
Of eating nothing else but rabbit,

And when he's finished, licks his paws
So's not to waste the onion sauce.)
A Cat's entitled to expect
These evidences of respect.
And so in time you reach your aim,
And finally call him by his NAME.

So this is this, and that is that:
And there's how you AD-DRESS A CAT.

Cat Morgan Introduces Himself

I once was a Pirate what sailed the 'igh seas —
   But now I've retired as a com-mission-aire:
And that's how you find me a-takin' my ease
   And keepin' the door in a Bloomsbury Square.

I'm partial to partridges, likewise to grouse,
   and I favour that Devonshire cream in a bowl;
But I'm allus content with a drink on the 'ouse
   And a bit o' cold fish when I done me patrol.

I ain't got much polish, me manners is gruff,
   But I've got a good coat, and I keep meself smart;
And everyone says, and I guess that's enough:
   'You can't but like Morgan, 'e's got a kind 'art.'

I got knocked about on the Barbary Coast,
   And me voice it ain't no sich melliferous horgan;
But yet I can state, and I'm not one to boast,
   That some of the gals is dead keen on old Morgan.

So if you 'ave business with Faber — or Faber —
   I'll give you this tip, and it's worth a lot more:
You'll save yourself time, and you'll spare yourself labour
   If jist you make friends with the Cat at the door.

MORGAN.